T0119406

Wild
Mocktails

Wild Mocktails

DELICIOUS MOCKTAILS USING HOME-GROWN AND FORAGED INGREDIENTS

Lottie Muir

CICO BOOKS
LONDON NEW YORK

This abridged edition published in 2019 by CICO Books
An imprint of Ryland Peters & Small Ltd
20–21 Jockey's Fields 341 E 116th St
London WC1R 4BW New York, NY 10029

www.rylandpeters.com

10 9 8 7 6 5 4 3 2 1

Material in this book is taken from the first edition of *Wild Mocktails* and from *Wild Cocktails from the Midnight Apothecary*.

A CIP catalog record for this book is available from the Library of Congress and the British Library.

ISBN: 978 1 78249 700 4

Printed in China

Editor: Dawn Bates
Designer: Eliana Holder
Photographer: Kim Lightbody
Art director: Sally Powell
Production controller: Mai-Ling Collyer
Publishing manager: Penny Craig
Publisher: Cindy Richards

Foraging wild ingredients requires expert knowledge and identification. The photographs and text in this book should not be used alone for identification purposes. The author and publisher cannot be held responsible for, nor shall be liable for, the erroneous consumption of wild plants that have caused severe or allergic reactions resulting from misidentification, nor the overconsumption of wild plants that have been shown to be toxic when consumed in large doses.

CONTENTS

INTRODUCTION

The choice to consume no alcohol is becoming more common, whether for health or religious reasons. Shortly after I made the semi-virtuous decision to include more mocktails and much less sugar in my diet, as well as in the menu at Midnight Apothecary, I went to a cocktail bar that served only non-alcoholic cocktails. Hoping to find the Holy Grail, I discovered that, although the drinks were delicious, some were overwhelmingly sweet and others reminded me of what I have for a healthy breakfast. Or they simply lacked the mouth-feel and va va voom that I consider vital for a cocktail.

Regardless of health, our Western palates are moving away from sweet and fruity toward drier, more aromatic, and bitter-forward drinks. The trend toward lower or no-alcohol serves reflects this. The trick is to dial down the sweetness, while still balancing the strong, bitter, sour, salt, and umami elements. This isn't straightforward. As with salt for a chef, "sugar" is still an important element in many drinks—not just for its sweetness, but also for its mouth-feel and flavor-extracting and preserving properties.

This new healthy foray has led me to discover other ways to play with the taste buds—from getting them just as stimulated with bitter or umami, as opposed to sweet sensations, to giving a drink viscosity with oil and proteins such as egg white (or canned chickpea/garbanzo bean water), as opposed to sugar. Where I have needed an additional sweet element in a cocktail, I have found an abundance of natural organic sweeteners that do the job beautifully and can be used in much smaller quantities than refined sugar.

I've found that it's about changing your approach to what you do with ingredients. So, whereas before I may have boiled up some herbs with a huge mound of refined sugar to make a syrup or added a massive dollop of sugar to them in some alcohol to make a liqueur, I have been more inclined to make an unsweetened tea. From the unsweetened tea, I can add further fresh aromatic or bitter herbs to the final drink and/or some type of water mixer and concentrated bitters that have further tiny elements of sweetness. With my unsweetened tea I can make a syrup with a tiny amount of natural sweetener such as maple syrup (which is a lot sweeter than sugar and therefore needed in smaller quantities); raw honey (which, although it contains sugar, is not refined and also has trace vitamins and minerals); or plants like sweet cicely or yacón fruit. Or I can play around with bitterness and aromatics using natural sweeteners. Bitters are a seasoning for drinks and are optional in a few of the recipes. They do contain tiny amounts of alcohol, but you'll find they really liven up a mocktail.

For many of us, the ethics surrounding our food and drink purchases are as important as our health choices. I don't want to consume coconut sugar as a healthy natural sweetener if it means a rainforest was razed to the ground to grow that particular brand. Or to have a natural sweetener flown from the other side of the world when I might get equally pleasing results from something growing near me, such as beets (beetroot) or yacón fruit. But what this means will obviously differ according to where you are reading this. If you're in California, for example, an organically produced raw agave syrup from Mexico is likely to have a lighter carbon footprint than if I were to buy it here in the U.K. And what I can buy here is more commonly a heavily chemically processed, fructose-packed version using the agave root, which doesn't do my health, pocket, or taste buds any good. The key is to find delicious, organic (if possible), ethically sourced ingredients that grow near you. If that's not always achievable, then hey, we can't always be saints.

What hasn't changed is the childlike pleasure to be gained from discovering ingredients that are literally growing all around you. Whether in your local street, park, hedgerow, or beach—or in your backyard or at a local farmers' market—these ingredients are about using amazing, organic, nutritious plants to give you enormous pleasure (and health benefits), as you get to know them intimately throughout the seasons and through their lifecycles.

To create these recipes, I invited other foragers and gardeners to share their recipes, using ingredients that are special to them. It meant visiting them in their own particular paradise and learning from them. Each has a vast array of knowledge and experience that they have generously shared. We share a desire to enjoy the plants growing among us for their profound benefits to our bodies, our minds, and the land around us.

I hope this book will be an opportunity to recharge your palate and get inventive in your desire for health and pleasure in a glass. Cheers!

EQUIPMENT

You will probably already have a lot of the tools and equipment listed here in your kitchen cupboards, especially if you enjoy cooking or making home-made drinks. However, if you are missing anything, these pieces are all available from good kitchen stores and online suppliers.

BASIC EQUIPMENT

You can improvise or supplement most equipment, but certain tools will make life easier and you're likely to already have, or be able to source, most of them easily and cheaply.

Blender This is great for making non-alcoholic, blended ice drinks. A top tip is to blend your ice first—to fully break it up—and then the liquids to ensure everything is blended smoothly.

Bottles and jars Hoard jars of every shape and size. Ideally, you need a range of sizes, including wide-mouthed, sealable, 1-quart (1-liter) glass jars such as Kilner or Mason jars. Little jelly (jam) jars and smaller jars are useful for tinctures and freezing herbs.

Coffee filters/AeroPress® coffee filter I use an AeroPress® one to ensure the clearest infusions with the fewest particles, but paper coffee filters do the same job as muslin or cheesecloth (when used with a fine-mesh strainer—see right) for avoiding sediment. I sometimes use a gold coffee filter when straining because it is reusable.

Coffee grinder For grinding spices, dried mushrooms, and all sorts.

Kilner jar

Fine-mesh strainer Like a chinois, this is for straining very small particles from infusions.

Funnel You need a funnel that is thinner than the top of your presentation bottle to get your infusion from the wide-mouthed pitcher into the finished bottle.

Glass presentation bottles Try to find a selection of bottles, ranging in size from ½ pint (250ml) to 1 quart (1 liter).

Heavy-bottomed, nonreactive saucepans It is important when you are using acidic ingredients, such as citrus juice and fruit, and strongly colored vegetables, to avoid pans made with aluminum, tin, or unlined copper—the pan lining will become stained and possibly pit and peel off.

Labels or pen You will get irritated very quickly if you cannot find a label or a pen that works on glass. Remember to always include the date and the contents on your bottled treasures.

Muslin/cheesecloth You really want to avoid sediment in the bottom of your creations because over time that organic matter festers. It also looks good to get it out. Several layers of clean muslin or cheesecloth inside a fine-mesh strainer can get your liquid as particle-free as it needs to be.

Wide-mouthed pitcher/jug Used for funneling infusions from a pan.

SPECIAL EQUIPMENT

These items are not essential—you can always improvise. However, they are fun, useful, and make mocktail-making tasks more enjoyable.

Barspoon This multipurpose tool fulfills a lot of different functions. It is designed to measure 1 barspoon (5ml). It stirs, mixes, muddles, and scoops, and is great for long glasses.

Blowtorch Catering blowtorches are great for jobs like grilling fruit or for scorching herbs to give a smoky taste to a mocktail.

Cocktail shaker There are several types of cocktail shaker. I prefer a Boston shaker, which is simply a pint-sized mixing glass with a slightly larger metal tin that fits on top. You will need a separate strainer. Alternatively, you can use a Cobbler shaker, which has an integrated strainer that is part of the lid, a tall glass, and a cap. Whichever shaker you buy, you simply fill the cocktail shaker two-thirds of the way up with ice, add your ingredients, cover, and shake. When the Boston shaker tin becomes frosty with condensation, your drink is cold enough to strain.

Cold-brew teapot Again, this is not essential but is designed to make your cold-brew tea very easy to make; there is a built-in filter so you don't have to strain your teas.

Cutting board and sharp knife Essential kit for prepping ingredients and garnishes.

Dehydrater These are useful for making garnishes. Borrow one from a friend, if need be.

Digital scales, pipettes, small dropper/apothecary bottles, and labels If you are interested in making bitters and tinctures, you will find a set of digital scales very useful for measuring the minute quantities that are needed. They are surprisingly cheap to buy. You will also need a pipette, small dropper or apothecary bottles, and labels for your final creations.

Hawthorne strainer This is the ideal strainer for a Boston shaker, as it is designed to fit over it perfectly. It is made of stainless steel with a spring-loaded coil around the perimeter to hold back ice and large particles of fruit or herbs as you pour into the cocktail glass. A top tip for making a foam using egg white is to put the spring-loaded coil into the cocktail shaker, seal, and shake. It really helps emulsify the mix and speeds up the time it takes to create a lovely foam.

Ice bucket and ice scoop/tongs If you're with close friends or family, you can probably omit these, but everyone else will expect you to use a scoop or some tongs for your cocktails. An ice bucket is useful for group gatherings.

Jigger This is used for pouring cocktails accurately. It is made of two "thimbles" that are joined together, with one thimble measuring 1oz (30ml), or a "pony shot," and the other measuring 1½oz (45ml), or a "standard" or "jigger" shot.

Julep strainer As the name suggests, this is the classic strainer for Juleps and is kept in the drink while you sip, to hold back the crushed ice. It basically looks like a domed metal spoon with holes in it. A julep strainer is also used to strain other drinks that are stirred in a mixing glass, as opposed to shaken.

Mixing glass A Boston shaker will already come with this glass, but there are plenty of attractive and/or vintage ones if you want to get fancy. A mixing glass of some sort is essential for drinks that need to be stirred, not shaken.

Muddler You can improvise with the disc end of a barspoon or the end of a wooden spoon, but a muddler is tall and skinny enough to fit in a long glass, yet wide enough to add some oomph when muddling fruit or herbs. Personally, I prefer to "smack" herbs to release their essential oils rather than bruise them with muddling (see page 12).

Jigger

Tea strainer Sometimes you need to double-strain your cocktail to catch tiny particles of ice, herbs, and fruit that won't be caught by the shaker's strainer or the hawthorne/ julep strainer. A regular tea strainer does the job nicely.

Tweezers/tongs Useful for handling edible flowers or herbs in long, thin glasses. The best type to get hold of are the long ones used by sushi/sous chefs, so you can reach the bottom of the glass.

GLASSWARE

Glassware doesn't just look good; it serves a purpose. For example, as plants feature heavily in garnishes in the long drinks, it's a good idea to use tall, thin Highball/Collins glasses that are not much wider than your ice cubes. This means you can stack the ice cubes on top of each other and push the flower and herb garnishes to the sides where they will be clearly visible—instead of them getting lost in the middle of the glass or sinking to the bottom.

I've suggested a glass for each of the mocktails in this book but you don't have to stick rigidly to those. Here's a guide to a range of glasses and the drinks—mainly cocktails—they are most commonly used for.

Balloon cup Increasingly, these large balloon cup or Copa de Balon glasses are the preferred choice for gin and tonic or even for spritz aperitifs, but they were traditionally used for red wine, allowing for maximum access to oxygen, and therefore maximum aroma and flavor. The glass is designed to trap the aromas of the gin to give a better taste to the drink, but the large bowl also allows plenty of ice and lime into the glass to add to the flavor and keep the drink cool. Crucially, though, the bowl shape is said to stop the ice cubes from melting too quickly.

Champagne flute Long, narrow-stemmed glass that is used to serve sparkling wine.

Collins/Highball These are perfect for serving long drinks over ice with a mixer. I try to use a 10-oz (300-ml) or 12-oz (360-ml) Collins glass for most long drinks.

Coupe/Saucer These are beautiful, bowl-shaped glasses, traditionally used for Champagne, but also great for Martinis, sours, and other cocktails. I prefer using a small 5-oz (150-ml) coupe glass.

Martini Also known as a cocktail glass, this is the classic cone-shaped glass with a stem. I use a 5-oz (150-ml) glass for most Martinis and sours.

Old Fashioned/Rocks These are great for serving Negronis or short drinks over ice—that is, "on the rocks." They are a short, wide, heavy bottomed glass in which you can use larger ice cubes to slow down the melting time.

Sherry Sherry glasses are smaller glasses that are great for reducing cocktail sizes generally. You can pick up gorgeous, mismatched vintage sherry glasses at thrift stores.

1 Wine glass
2 Champagne flute
3 Balloon cup
4 Highball
5 Collins
6 Rocks
7 Martini
8 Sherry

TECHNIQUES

Whether you are a complete novice at mixing drinks or have a little experience, following the techniques outlined here will help you to become more proficient and create the best-tasting mocktails. With practice, these techniques will soon become second nature.

MEASURING

If you wish, you can work in "parts" rather than ounces or milliliters to work out ratios. Whichever method you choose, it's a good idea for balance and consistency to measure accurately, especially when you devise a recipe you want to repeat. Making the smallest changes can knock a recipe out.

MUDDLING

If you don't have a muddler, you can use the disc end of a barspoon or the end of a wooden spoon instead. Muddling lightly crushes ingredients like citrus or other fruits to release their juices. Muddling can bruise some ingredients, however, releasing unwanted bitterness into a drink, so I prefer to "smack" herbs in the palm of my hand to release their essential oils before dropping them into the cocktail shaker or mixing glass.

Shaking

SHAKING

If your drink contains citrus, or liquids that have a wide variety of viscosity (e.g. a thin spirit and a thick syrup, or dairy or chickpea/garbanzo bean water), you need to shake your drink. Shaking thoroughly combines the ingredients, so you don't get layered flavors and textures. It also makes your drink colder and more diluted.

Fill a shaker two-thirds of the way up with ice. Add the ingredients, seal the shaker, and shake hard for 20 seconds. If you are using egg white or chickpea water, either shake harder for another 10 seconds or, alternatively, take the coiled spring from a hawthorne strainer and drop it into the mocktail mix before sealing and shaking—this will help emulsify the mix in a regular 20-second shake. Remember to put the spring back on the hawthorne strainer before straining and serving!

STERILIZING

Wash bottles and jars, and other pieces of equipment that need sterilizing, in very hot, soapy water, then dry them in an oven set to a low temperature. Alternatively, you can use some sterilizing solution/tablets, following the manufacturer's instructions on the label. This method is ideal for sterilizing equipment such as metal or wooden utensils. Either way, you are probably using organic ingredients, so it's important that your storage jars and bottles are sterilized before use.

STIRRING

Pour the ingredients into a regular mixing glass or the metal half of a Boston shaker. Fill the mixing glass two-thirds of the way up with ice. Use a long-handled barspoon or the handle of a wooden spoon to stir the ingredients for about 20 seconds or until condensation appears on the outside of the glass. Strain and serve.

Mixing glass

STRAINING

To serve a clear, particle-free mocktail, place a strainer over the mouth of the shaker or mixing glass to hold back the ice and any pieces of fruit and herbs, while you pour the liquid into the glass.

Fine-straining When you're bottling infusions it is important to keep them as particle- and sediment-free as possible, to preserve their flavor, shelf life, and looks. Rather than just using a kitchen sieve, a fine-mesh strainer, such as a chinois, can be placed over a wide-mouthed pitcher or jar and a few layers of muslin/cheesecloth placed inside to catch the smallest particles. Alternatively, you can line the fine-mesh strainer with coffee filters, passing the infusion through them to achieve equally great results.

Double-straining To double-strain, place a strainer over the mouth of the shaker or mixing glass held in one hand, while holding a tea strainer in the other hand directly over the cocktail glass. Pour the mix through the main strainer and also through the tea strainer to double-strain/catch any remaining ice particles or pieces of herb and fruit.

DRYING HERBS

To dry soft herbs swiftly, place the freshly picked herbs in a single layer on a baking sheet. Place in an oven heated to the lowest possible setting until the herbs are brittle or crumble easily (check them regularly). You can even leave the door open if you don't mind overheating yourself! Store the dried herbs in a cool, dry place away from sunlight, moisture, and heat. Most dried herbs diminish in flavor after a year.

Note: All fruit/vegetable/plant/herb ingredients should be washed before use, particularly foraged plants.

The Skinny on the Sweet

You may not consciously think of bitters, tonic water, or an innocent-looking strawberry as containing sugars but they are, of course, packed with them in different forms and quantities. Even wine and spirits, such as vodka and gin, have a tiny amount of fructose. However, just as salt and pepper are vital seasonings for a chef, so too is sweetness in some form essential for a mocktail-maker to balance bitter and herbal flavors.

Refined sugar is processed, bleached, lacks any nutrients, and, in excess, overloads our insulin-producing pancreas and liver to a point where neither can cope and serious health problems may ensue. Many people are now looking to replace refined sugar in their diets with "healthy sweeteners." However, there is a gray area surrounding what constitutes a healthy sweetener. With this in mind, I'd like to highlight the six key facts on which I've based my choice of sweeteners:

* An element of sweetness is necessary in nearly every mocktail.
* Most sugars, whether in plants and honey or in a refined processed state, contain a mix of glucose and fructose in differing proportions.
* Glucose is an essential molecule for life and, in a healthy diet, is very easily metabolized by the body to provide the energy we need to survive.
* Fructose, which is found naturally in fruit and honey, is easily digested in small quantities as part of a healthy diet. In large quantities, however, it puts a strain on the liver and can lead to major health problems.
* Highly processed sweeteners, even those based on nutrient-rich plants or honey, lose nutritional benefits if they are heated to a high temperature.
* Unprocessed sweeteners that have been flown thousands of miles around the world and/or grown on rainforest or pristine land razed to create that yield are unethical, even if they are packed with nutritional benefits.

In a healthy diet, in which the majority of the food intake is fresh, unprocessed food such as vegetables, fruit, nuts, seeds, and wholegrains (i.e. complex carbohydrates), every cell in the body is happy to metabolize starches and convert them into glucose to provide energy. Fructose (also found naturally in fruit, vegetables, and honey) can be converted too but, in contrast, only liver cells can break it down. This is fine in small quantities because the foodstuffs containing fructose also come with a host of beneficial vitamins, antioxidants, and fiber, and a healthy body has a fully functioning pancreas and liver to manage the process. Difficulties arise because, in our processed-food culture, we have gone from consuming an average of ½oz (15g) of fructose per day in the early 1900s, mostly from fruit and vegetables, to nearly 2oz (55g) today. There has been a parallel rise in levels of obesity and diabetes, as well as the emergence of a new condition called non-alcoholic fatty liver disease. This is because one of the end products of processing fructose in the liver is triglyceride, a form of fat. Uric acid and free radicals are also formed. Triglycerides can damage liver function and contribute to a buildup of fatty plaques in the arteries. Free radicals can damage cell structures, enzymes, and even genes. Uric acid can also turn off the production of nitric oxide, a substance that helps protect artery walls from damage. Another effect of a high-fructose intake is insulin resistance, which can be a precursor to diabetes.

However, it's not all bad news. History has taught us that moderation is key, our bodies are amazing, and plants are our allies. By relearning the medicinal benefits of the herbs known to our ancestors, we can enjoy a small amount of natural sugar and a lot of beneficial plant life in some delicious and healthy drinks! There are a few basic rules of thumb if you wish to lower your sugar intake, stay healthy, and have a balanced and delicious drink. Where possible, use sparkling water in place of tonic waters, fruit juices, and other mixers. When deciding on the sweet element to use in a drink, opt for sweet ingredients that also have added health benefits.

There should be several local, sustainable sweet alternatives available to you that are both healthy and delicious in small quantities. These might include beets (beetroot), raw honey, dates, figs, grapes, sweet herbs (such as sweet cicely), bee pollen, pine pollen, and whole fruit.

Avoid using agave nectar, if possible. It is marketed as a "healthy sweetener" because it is high in fructose (up to 97 percent) and low on the glycemic index, but it is, in fact, no such thing. Fructose in small quantities as part of a healthy diet is fine, but it is only low on the glycemic index because it is processed in the liver. Finally, while the agave plant may have antioxidant and anti-inflammatory properties, the high-temperature processing and additions made to most commercial agave products remove those benefits. Even the inulin in fructose—a good source of fiber—is destroyed in the process.

On the other hand, raw coconut nectar (or coconut palm nectar) is meant to be healthy for the opposite reason: it is very low in fructose (about 10 percent) and produced at low temperatures to preserve its health-giving properties. Formed from the sweet sap tapped from flowering coconut blossom stems, it is organic, raw (so the enzymes are still active), and packed with amino acids and quite a few vitamins and minerals. It may, however, have traveled long distances. Personally, I am uncomfortable with the sustainability of such crops and whether they need to be transported from the other side of the world when more local healthy alternatives are available. Some argue that coconut nectar is environmentally friendly because coconut palms produce 50–75 percent more sugar per acre than sugar cane. Despite this, I still prefer to use something from closer to home.

Beet, Cacao Nib, & Yacón Syrup MOCKTAIL

Beet (beetroot) and chocolate are natural bedfellows. The cacao nibs give a surprising level of bitterness, but the beet is naturally sweet. I have suggested using a drop of yacón syrup, mainly for mouth-feel, but also to provide a pleasant sweetness that pairs well with the other ingredients. The syrup will not discolor the drink because the beet is so dark. I like to top this up with a dose of birch sap and a dash of sparkling water—add extra sparkling water if you don't have any birch sap.

* 1 tsp raw cacao nibs
* 2oz (60ml) beet (beetroot) juice
* 2 tsp (10ml) yacón syrup
* 2oz (60ml) birch sap (see page 52)
* 2 dashes of Bittermens Xocolatl Mole Bitters (optional)
* Splash of sparkling water

* **Tools:** Muddler, cocktail shaker with strainer, tea strainer
* **Glass:** Rocks
* **Ice:** Cubes
* **Garnish:** Nasturtium flower, *Anchusa azurea* 'Lodden Royalist,' and blackcurrant sage (*Salvia microphylla*) leaf

Serves 1

Nasturtium

Tip the cacao nibs into the bottom of the cocktail shaker. Use the muddler to crush the nibs and release their flavor. Fill the shaker two-thirds of the way up with ice. Add all the other ingredients (except the sparkling water). Shake vigorously, then double-strain (see page 13) into the rocks glass to catch the nibs and add the splash of sparkling water. Garnish with your choice of herbaceous or spicy flowers and edible greenery. I've used a yellow nasturtium flower, a blackcurrant sage leaf, and a sprig of blue *Anchusa azurea* 'Lodden Royalist.'

Roast Quince, Szechuan Pepper, Juniper, & Star Anise MOCKTAIL

When there is a seasonal glut of well-paired ingredients, such as quince and Szechuan pepper, it's a shame not to max out their potential in all kinds of foods and drinks. You can roast quince to make a dessert and then use the leftover juices in this mocktail. (Please note the Citrus Bitters contain a tiny amount of alcohol.)

* ¼ cup (50ml) Roast Quince Juice (see opposite)
* 1oz (30ml) apple and rhubarb juice, apple juice, or pear juice (or apple verjuice if you have any)
* ¼ cup (50ml) sparkling water, birch sap (see page 52), or tonic water (whichever your prefer)
* 2 dashes of Citrus Bitters (see page 46, optional)

* **Tools:** Mixing glass, barspoon/long spoon, strainer
* **Glass:** Highball/rocks
* **Ice:** Cubes
* **Garnish:** Roasted quince segment

Serves 1

Fill the mixing glass two-thirds of the way up with ice, add the Roast Quince Juice and your choice of fruit juice, then stir well to chill down the drink. Strain the mocktail into the serving glass, top up with your choice of sparkling water/birch sap/tonic water, and add the Citrus Bitters (if using). Garnish with a segment of roasted quince.

Roast Quince JUICE

This recipe provides enough juice to make two mocktails.

* 1 large quince, peeled and cut into slim, ½-in (1-cm) chunks
* 7 Szechuan peppercorns
* 7 juniper berries
* 1 star anise
* 5oz (150ml) pear or apple juice (or apple verjuice if you have any)
* ¼ cup (50ml) maple syrup
* Freshly squeezed juice of ½ lemon
* 3 x 1-in (2.5-cm) pieces of lemon zest

* **Tools:** Small roasting pan, fine-mesh strainer, measuring pitcher

To roast the quince, preheat the oven to 180°C/350°F/Gas 4. Place the peeled and chopped quince, Szechuan peppercorns, juniper berries, star anise, pear juice, maple syrup, and lemon juice and zest in the roasting pan. Stir well to coat the quince.

Roast for 30 minutes, stirring occasionally to make sure nothing sticks to the pan. Remove and let cool before straining ⅓ cup (100ml) of the cooled liquid into the pitcher (see page 13), ready for making your mocktails.

Roasted quince

Strawberry & Lemon Verbena MOCKTAIL

Using strawberries, lemon verbena (*Aloysia citrodora*) leaves, and sweet cicely (*Myrrhis odorata*) seeds, this mocktail really is a taste of summer—grown-up, herbaceous, and with enough sweetness for you to indulge yourself. Adding a splash of bitters, which contain a small amount of alcohol, is optional.

* 5 ripe strawberries, washed and hulled
* 5 lemon verbena leaves
* 5 sweet cicely seeds
* 2 tsp (10ml) freshly squeezed lemon juice
* Grind of coarse black pepper
* 4oz (120ml) sparkling water
* 2 dashes of Citrus Bitters (see page 46) or orange bitters (optional)

* **Tools:** Cocktail shaker with strainer, muddler, barspoon/mixing rod
* **Glass:** Champagne/rocks/wine
* **Ice:** Cubes
* **Garnish:** Sweet cicely seeds and leaf, lemon verbena leaf

Serves 1

Fill the serving glass with ice. Place the strawberries, lemon verbena leaves, and sweet cicely seeds in the bottom of the cocktail shaker and muddle thoroughly (see page 12) to release all the juices, essential oils, and flavors. Add the lemon juice and black pepper. Fill the shaker two-thirds of the way up with ice. Seal and shake hard for 20 seconds to really muddle things up and cool things down. Strain the mocktail into the serving glass. Top up with sparkling water, add the bitters (if using), and stir to combine. Garnish with sweet cicely seeds, if you wish, a sweet cicely leaf, and a lemon verbena leaf.

Roast Rhubarb, Blood Orange, Sweet Cicely, & Lemongrass MOCKTAIL

Like the mocktail on page 18, this recipe involves straining off the delicious juices from a potential dessert, letting them cool, and sticking them in a glass. I have given two options for the mixer: you can either use ginger ale and sparkling water or, if you have a juicer, try topping up the drink with fresh rhubarb juice and adding a dash of sparkling water to give some fizz. Four or five stalks of rhubarb will provide ⅓ cup (100ml) juice.

* ¼ cup (50ml) Roast Rhubarb Juice (see opposite)
* ⅔oz (20ml) ginger ale and ¼ cup (50ml) sparkling water or ¼ cup (50ml) freshly juiced raw rhubarb and ⅔oz (20ml) sparkling water
* Squeeze of fresh lemon
* **Tools:** Juicer (optional), mixing glass, barspoon/long spoon, tea strainer
* **Glass:** Highball
* **Ice:** Cubes
* **Garnish:** Sweet cicely leaf and/or blood orange segment

Serves 1

Fill the mixing glass two-thirds of the way up with ice. Add the Roast Rhubarb Juice, ginger ale/ fresh rhubarb juice (whichever you are using), and squeeze of lemon. Stir well to chill the drink properly. Strain into the serving glass, using a tea strainer to catch any bits, and top with the correct measure of sparkling water. Garnish with a sweet cicely leaf and/ or a segment of blood orange.

Roast Rhubarb JUICE

This recipe provides enough juice to make two mocktails.

* 4–5 stalks of rhubarb, cut into 1-in (2.5-cm) chunks
* 3 x 2-in (5-cm) pieces of orange peel
* 3 sprigs of sweet cicely leaves
* 1 finely chopped lemongrass stalk (outer layers removed)
* 5oz (150ml) blood orange juice (or regular orange juice if you prefer)

* **Tools:** Small ovenproof skillet or frying pan, fine-mesh strainer, measuring pitcher

To roast the rhubarb, preheat the oven to 180°C/350°F/Gas 4. Put the rhubarb and other ingredients in the skillet or frying pan, and cover with the blood orange juice. Roast for about 40 minutes, stirring occasionally to prevent the rhubarb sticking or drying out. Remove from the oven, let cool, and strain ⅓ cup (100ml) of the juices into the pitcher, ready for making your mocktails.

Roasting rhubarb

Sea Buckthorn & Fermented Birch Sap MOCKTAIL

This mocktail is oozing zeitgeist health and coolness, but, in spite of itself, it's delicious! Sea buckthorn (*Hippophae rhamnoides*) is found growing everywhere, not just at the coast, so you can either make your own juice from wild berries (see opposite) or source it from reputable online suppliers. The berries are bursting with vitamin C, antioxidants, and omega oils, and are even high in protein. They have plenty of sourness, but none of the bitterness of citrus fruit. The naturally sweetened Fermented Birch Sap provides just the right amount of healthy sweetness to take the edge off, as well as adding more complexity and goodness.

* 1 cup (250ml) Fresh Sea Buckthorn Juice (see opposite) or store-bought sea buckthorn juice
* 1 cup (250ml) Fermented Birch Sap (see page 52)

* **Tools:** Barspoon/long spoon
* **Glass:** Highball (x 4)
* **Ice:** Cubes
* **Garnish:** Flowering sprig of Darwin's barberry (*Berberis darwinii*)

Serves 4 (makes approximately 1 pint/500ml)

Fill 4 highball glasses with ice. Pour 2oz (60ml) of sea buckthorn juice into each glass. Add the Fermented Birch Sap (about 2oz/60ml per serve) until it reaches the tops of the glasses, and stir. A cluster of Darwin's barberry flowers finishes the drink with an exquisite, tropical, sweet garnish.

FRESH SEA BUCKTHORN JUICE

The hellish thorns make harvesting sea buckthorn berries difficult. A good tip is to cut off whole branches covered in berries (you'll get about 12in/30cm of berries per branch) and freeze them, so you can just knock or shake the berries off and save yourself a world of pain and frustration. From four 12-in (30-cm) branches full of berries you will have enough juice to make four mocktails. Simply put the branches in a sealable container or plastic bag and keep them in the freezer for at least a couple of hours. Once the berries have frozen, knock or shake them into a large bowl and leave them to thaw fully. Use a potato masher to push or squeeze the juice out of the berries. Fine-strain the juice (see page 13) into a measuring pitcher, ready to make your mocktails.

Vegan & Virgin PIÑA COLADA

This really is a delicious mocktail to have morning, noon, or night. I am aware that coconuts have a high carbon footprint for me living in the U.K., but plenty of people enjoy a bounty of coconuts on their doorstep. Lucky them!

* ¼ cup (100g) organic young coconut meat (canned is fine)
* 1 cup (250g) frozen pineapple chunks
* 2 tsp (10ml) freshly squeezed lime juice
* 1 tsp (5ml) honey
* ½ cup (125ml) Coconut Milk Kefir (see page 51)

* **Tools:** Food blender
* **Glass:** Highball/dessert
* **Ice:** Cubes
* **Garnish:** Pineapple chunk and/or pineapple weed (*Matricaria discoidea*) flower/leaf

Serves 1

Add all the ingredients (apart from the Coconut Milk Kefir) to the food blender and blend for 10 seconds on high. Add the Coconut Milk Kefir and blend on low for a further 5 seconds. Pop 3 ice cubes in the serving glass, pour in the mix, and garnish with a pineapple chunk and/or pineapple weed flower/leaf. Enjoy!

Coconut Water Kefir
STRAWBERRY COSMO

The slightly fizzy, tart Coconut Water Kefir tastes delicious with strawberries (though you will find it mixes with endless combinations of juices or smoothies), and provides a level of complexity that will make your mocktails taste both grown-up and interesting.

* 1oz (30ml) Coconut Water Kefir (see page 49)
* ½ cup (65g) strawberries
* 1 cup (250ml) chilled sparkling water
* Squeeze of fresh lime

* **Tools**: Food blender
* **Glass:** Martini
* **Ice:** Cubes
* **Garnish:** Strawberry segment and basil sprig

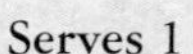

Serves 1

Put the Coconut Kefir Water and strawberries in the freezer for 30 minutes to chill, then place in the food blender and blend until smooth. Add the chilled sparkling water and a squeeze of lime, and pulse for a moment more. Pour the contents into the iced-filled Martini glass, and garnish with a segment of strawberry and a basil sprig.

Fruity & Flowery SUMMER MOCKTAIL

This delicious mocktail draws on the summery sweetness of red clover (*Trifolium pratense*) and meadowsweet (*Filipendula ulmaria*) flowers. I have suggested adding a dash of bitters, which contain a tiny amount of alcohol, but these are optional.

* ⅔oz (20ml) Strawberry, Clover, & Meadowsweet Shrub (see page 54)
* ⅓ cup (100ml) sparkling water
* Dash of Citrus Bitters (see page 46) or orange bitters (optional)

* **Tools**: Barspoon/long spoon
* **Glass:** Highball/rocks
* **Ice:** Cubes
* **Garnish:** Red clover blossom and meadowsweet buds

Serves 1

Fill the highball or rocks glass with ice. Pour the Strawberry, Clover, & Meadowsweet Shrub into the glass. Top with the sparkling water and add a dash of your chosen bitters, if desired. Stir well and garnish with red clover blossom and meadowsweet buds.

Lilac & Nettle MOCKTAIL

Lilac (*Syringa vulgaris*) is one of those heady, floral wonders that fills streets and parks with the unmistakeable scent of spring. To preserve as much of the flavor as possible, I have suggested something akin to a quick, cold-brewed tea. Young nettle (*Urtica dioica*) tips are bursting with detoxifying goodness and give drinks a wonderful tannic quality. Put the two together with a drop of honey and you've got yourself a gorgeous springtime sipper!

* 5oz (150ml) Lilac & Nettle Tea (see opposite)
* Squeeze of fresh lemon
* 2 tsp (10ml) honey or maple syrup

* **Tools:** Cocktail shaker with strainer
* **Glass:** Rocks
* **Ice:** Cubes
* **Garnish**: Lilac blossoms

Serves 1

Fill the rocks glass with ice and fill the cocktail shaker two-thirds of the way up with ice. Add the Lilac & Nettle Tea, squeeze of lemon, and your choice of syrup. Shake well and strain into the rocks glass. Garnish with lilac blossoms.

Lilac & Nettle
TEA

This recipe provides enough tea to make five mocktails.

* 2 packed cups (about 4 handfuls) of lilac flowers (all greenery removed)
* 1 packed cup (about 2 handfuls) of young nettle leaves
* 3 cups (750ml) boiling water
* Freshly squeezed juice of ½ lemon
* 1 tsp (5ml) honey or maple syrup

* **Tools:** Small nonreactive saucepan, fine mesh strainer, measuring pitcher

Lilac

Put the lilac flowers and nettle leaves in the nonreactive saucepan and add enough boiling water (about 3 cups/750ml) to cover the plant material. While the water is still hot, add the lemon juice and your choice of syrup, and stir. Allow the tea to cool naturally and leave for at least 2 hours and a maximum of 4 hours before straining (see page 13) into the pitcher, ready to make your mocktails.

Lavender HONEYSUCKLE

You can make this summer mocktail punch in quantity in advance and then top up everyone's glass with soda water on the day. As well as tasting delicious, it is also very good for you. Raw honey is rich in cancer-fighting phytonutrients and powerful antioxidants, found in the propolis that the bees use to sterilize the beehive. The acacia blossoms provide extra floral notes but aren't strictly necessary.

* 2 cups (640g) raw, runny honey
* 2 cups (500ml) warm water
* 2 heaped tbsp fresh edible-grade lavender buds or 4 tsp dried lavender blossoms
* 2 heads of acacia blossom (optional, if in season)
* 1 cup (250ml) freshly squeezed lemon juice
* 2 lemons, sliced into thin wheels
* 1 cup (20g) lemon balm (*Melissa officinalis*) or mint (*Mentha*) leaves
* Splash of soda water

Serves 6 (makes approximately 1½ pints/750ml

* **Tools:** Large nonreactive pan, wooden spoon, fine-mesh strainer and muslin/cheesecloth or coffee filter, ladle (optional)
* **Glass:** Collins (x 6)
* **Ice:** Cubes
* **Garnish:** Lavender sprigs, mint, or lemon balm sprigs

Combine the honey and water in the nonreactive pan and stir over a low heat until the honey liquefies and dissolves. Just before the liquid boils, add the lavender buds and acacia blossom heads (if you have them), remove the pan from the heat, and let steep for 20 minutes.

Fine-strain the mixture (see page 13) into a large pitcher to remove the lavender buds (and blossoms). Return the liquid to the cleaned pan, then add the lemon juice and the lemon wheels. Smack the lemon balm or mint leaves between your palms to release the essential oils. Add to the pan. Let stand for an hour.

If you wish, strain the mocktail punch again. Alternatively, remove the lemon balm or mint leaves and serve using a ladle, as we do at Midnight Apothecary. Fill 6 glasses with ice. Pour the punch two-thirds of the way up each glass. Top with a splash of soda water. Garnish with the sprigs of lavender and fresh sprigs of mint or lemon balm.

If you don't pick the lavender yourself, make sure that you buy "edible grade" lavender, which has been handled hygienically.

Regal Mary MOCKTAIL

Try mixing some Beet Kvass (see opposite) with Water Kefir to make this virgin Bloody Mary. Don't serve this mocktail over ice because that will water it down too much and make the kvass frothy when you shake it. Instead, "roll" the mocktail, which cools down the drink without the frothiness.

* 1 cup (250ml) Water Kefir (see page 48)
* 2oz (60ml) Beet Kvass (see opposite) or tomato juice
* 1oz (30ml) celery juice
* 1 tsp (5ml) freshly squeezed lemon juice
* Pinch of sea salt
* Pinch of black pepper
* Dash of hot Tabasco
* 2 dashes of Bittermens Xocolatl Mole Bitters (optional)

* **Tools:** Measuring pitcher, barspoon/wooden spoon, 2 mixing glasses, cocktail shaker with strainer
* **Glass:** Collins
* **Ice:** Cubes
* **Garnish:** Lovage/celery/fennel stalk and nasturtium leaves and flowers (if available)

Serves 1

Add all the ingredients to the pitcher and stir. Fill one of the mixing glasses two-thirds of the way up with ice. Pour the mix into the mixing glass and immediately "roll" (or transfer) the whole mix, including the ice, into the other mixing glass. Repeat this process, back and forth between the two mixing glasses, until your drink is cold. Strain immediately into the Collins glass, garnish with a lovage/celery/fennel stalk and nasturtium leaves and flowers, and serve.

Beet Kvass

This fermented beet (beetroot) juice is packed with probiotics and enzymes. It makes a salty and earthy contribution to a virgin or alcoholic Bloody Mary—try using it as a substitute for tomato juice in the Regal Mary Mocktail (see opposite). Alternatively, mix it with an earthy spirit, such as mezcal or tequila, to make a delicious cocktail.

* 2 large or 4 small organic beets (beetroot), washed (peeled first if non-organic)
* ¼ cup (50ml) whey (the strained liquid from full-fat plain yogurt) or lacto-fermented pickle juice (from a commercial jar of sauerkraut)
* 1 tbsp sea salt
* 1 quart (1 liter) filtered (chlorine-free) water

Tools

* 1-quart (1-liter) wide-mouthed jar, sterilized (see page 12)
* Fermentation cover (such as a clean piece of cotton/closely woven dishtowel/T-shirt or coffee filter) and rubber band
* Fine-mesh strainer and muslin/cheesecloth or coffee filter
* Sealable presentation bottle(s), sterilized

Makes approximately 1 quart (1 liter)

Chop the beet/beetroot into ½-in (1-cm) cubes and put in the sterilized jar. Add the whey or pickle juice and salt, then pour in the filtered water. Cover with the fermentation cover and secure with a rubber band. Leave at room temperature for 2 days in a cupboard or on a countertop away from direct sunlight until the mix has fermented. Fine-strain the kvass (see page 13) into a wide-mouthed pitcher, funnel into the sterilized presentation bottle(s), seal, and store in the refrigerator. Consume within 3 months.

Birch, Ginger, & WISTERIA DETOXER

This mocktail is a great detoxer. Sap from the white birch (*Betula alba*) or silver birch (*Betula pendula*) is one of the healthiest juices you can drink. Unless you know how to harvest it yourself, online is your best place to source it. First impressions aren't good, though. It's a thin, slightly sweet, slightly bitter, herbal watery liquid, but its restorative and detoxifying properties are legendary. Unusually, it tackles the body's two cleansing and purification systems—the liver and kidneys—at the same time, and helps flush out harmful toxins, uric acid, and excess water from the body.

Its partner here is flavorsome ginger, with its own health-giving properties. Ginger fires up the digestive juices and, according to Ayurvedic texts, the libido! It also clears the sinuses, overcomes nausea and flatulence, and contains anti-inflammatory properties. Meanwhile, the wisteria flower garnish has a role here primarily for its looks—it's really pretty and the perfect blowzy opposite to the restrained, cloudy-looking tonic. It's also edible.

* 3oz (90ml) birch sap (see page 52)
* 1oz (30ml) Ginger Syrup (see page 57)
* ¾oz (22ml) freshly squeezed lemon juice
* Splash of soda water

* **Tools:** Cocktail shaker with strainer
* **Glass:** Collins
* **Ice:** Cubes
* **Garnish:** Wisteria blossom

Serves 1

Chill the glass thoroughly in the freezer or refrigerator for 2 or 4 hours respectively. Alternatively, fill the glass with ice.

Pour all the ingredients into the cocktail shaker and fill it two-thirds of the way up with ice. Cover and shake hard for 20 seconds. If you used ice to chill your glass, empty it out. Strain the cocktail into the glass. Garnish with the wisteria blossom and top with a splash of soda water.

Birch sap is high in potassium, calcium, phosphorus, magnesium, manganese, zinc, sodium, iron, and copper, not to mention vitamins B and C. On the down side, it has a very short shelf life (2–5 days), even if refrigerated, but it does freeze well.

Only THE MAHONIA

This dark, vaguely honey-scented syrup makes a wonderful mocktail. It could be called a Julep—it certainly looks like one and it's made in a julep cup and with a julep strainer—but, strictly speaking, that would be wrong, in part because we've chosen to make it non-alcoholic, using grape juice. The julep cup, though, is the perfect show-off vessel for draping over bunches of mahonia berries, bringing to mind an Ancient Greek bacchanalian feast.

- 1½oz (45ml) Mahonia Syrup (see page 59)
- ¾oz (22ml) freshly squeezed lime juice
- 5 mint leaves
- 2oz (60ml) red or white grape juice

- **Tools:** Cocktail shaker with strainer, julep strainer
- **Glass:** Chilled julep cup
- **Ice:** Cubes, crushed
- **Garnish:** Raceme of mahonia berries, preferably Oregon grape (*Mahonia aquifolium*)

Serves 1

Pour the Mahonia Syrup and lime juice into the cocktail shaker, fill it two-thirds of the way up with ice cubes, and shake hard for 20 seconds. Smack a mint leaf between your palms to release the essential oil and rub it around the edge of the chilled julep cup. Place it in the cup. Smack the remaining 4 mint leaves and place in the cup. Fill with crushed ice. Strain the mahonia and lime mix through the crushed ice in the glass to combine and further chill the drink. Top with red or white grape juice until just below the top of the crushed ice. Place the julep strainer inside the cup and garnish with the raceme of mahonia berries.

This cocktail is yet another appetite stimulator and booster of the immune system, but is to be avoided if you are pregnant or breast-feeding because of its uterine-stimulating properties.

Mahonia berries are high in vitamin C and, in the past, they were often used to treat scurvy. The alkaloids in them have been found to be antibacterial, antifungal, anti-inflammatory, antioxidant, and antidiarrheal.

Mahonia pairs beautifully with milder fruit like apples, pears, and grapes.

Red Clover LEMONADE

The beautiful flowers of red clover (*Trifolium pratense*) are slightly sweet, and many of us will have enjoyed them in clover honey. They are also packed with nutrients, calcium, magnesium, potassium, and vitamin C. Red clover has been used in tea form for many years to alleviate the symptoms of gout. This lemonade is a quick and easy recipe that leaves you with a very pretty, delicately flavored sweet drink—think sweet hay.

- 3 cups (750ml) water
- Approximately 40 red clover blossoms
- 1 cup (250ml) freshly squeezed lemon juice
- 3 tbsp (50ml) honey, preferably raw, set or runny
- Soda water

- **Tools:** Small nonreactive pan, fine-mesh strainer and muslin/cheesecloth or coffee filter, wooden spoon
- **Glass:** Collins (x 6)
- **Ice:** Cubes
- **Garnish:** Red clover blossoms

Serves 6 (approximately 1 quart/1 liter)

Bring the water to a slow boil in the nonreactive pan, add the clover blossoms, and gently simmer for 5 minutes. Fine-strain the liquid (see page 13) into the wide-mouthed pitcher, removing the blossoms, and return to the cleaned pan over a low heat. Add the lemon juice and honey, and stir to dissolve the honey. Do not let it boil. Remove from the heat and pour the lemonade into the cleaned pitcher. Chill for a couple of hours in the refrigerator.

To serve, fill the 6 glasses with ice. Pour the lemonade three-quarters of the way up each one. Garnish with fresh red clover blossoms. Top with soda water and serve immediately.

Coumarin, the slightly vanilla-flavored phytochemical present in red clover, has antifungal and antitumor properties, but it also thins the blood. While that may be great for some, people taking anticoagulants should not consume red clover in large quantities.

Many menopausal women who experience hot flashes (flushes) take red clover in some form because it is considered to be one of the highest sources of isoflavones, which act like estrogens.

Violet TEA

I am lucky in my area of London, as there are carpets of violets in a patch of local woodland. All species of wild violet are edible and medicinally valuable, but the scent of *Viola odorata* is more accented. You can make this tea using fresh or dried leaves and flowers—the flavor will be stronger if you dry them first (see Drying Herbs, page 13) but sometimes it's more fun to have instant gratification from your fresh bounty.

- 7oz (200ml) boiling water
- 2–3 tsp fresh violet flowers and finely torn leaves or 1–2 tsp dried violet flowers and leaves (dried, organic, and unsprayed)
- Honey, to taste (optional)
- Squeeze of fresh lemon (optional)

- **Tools:** Heatproof measuring pitcher, teapot (optional), teaspoon, tea strainer, serving cup(s)

Makes 1 cup (approximately ⅓ pint/200ml)

Pour 7oz (200ml) of boiling water per serve over the violet flowers and leaves in either the pitcher or teapot (depending on the quantity you are making). Steep for 5 minutes. Let cool, strain into your serving cup(s), and serve with some honey and lemon (if using).

Both the leaves and flowers of violets are a medicinal and nutritional powerhouse—the leaves are bitter, but the flowers are sweet and tangy. They are loaded with vitamins A and C. In fact, two small violet leaves fulfill our daily requirement of vitamin C!

As far back as 1885, a study showed that the leaves, if collected in spring, contain twice as much vitamin C as the same weight of oranges and more than twice the amount of vitamin A, gram for gram, as spinach. They were traditionally used as a blood purifier to be consumed at the end of winter to stimulate the lymphatic glands, eliminate toxins, and generally boost our immune systems and energize us for spring. The other great thing about violets is their color. They produce a gorgeous purple drink that turns cerise when mixed with an acid… all very cool!

Blackcurrant Sage, Winter Savory, & Lemon Verbena TEA

Blackcurrant sage (*Salvia microphylla*) produces a profusion of gorgeous scarlet flowers, which makes it a great plant for providing a garnish. But it is the amazing leaves that set it apart as a fantastic addition to a cocktail garden. The plant originates from South America and the leaves can be used fresh or dried, alongside the flowers, in a famous tea called *mirot de montes*, or "myrtle of the mountains," to treat fever. Here I've steeped it with some winter savory (*Satureja montana*), which can be used like thyme, but I think gives notes of pine, thyme, and pepper in one plant. The lemon verbena (*Aloysia citrodora*) offers up an exquisite lemony sweetness, but is one of those plants to use sparingly as it is very strong.

- 7oz (200ml) boiling water
- 3 tsp fresh or 1 tsp dried blackcurrant sage or small handful of fresh blackcurrant (*Ribes nigrum*) leaves
- 4 lemon verbena leaves
- 2-in (5-cm) winter savory sprig

- **Tools:** Heatproof measuring pitcher, teapot (optional), teaspoon, tea strainer, serving cup(s)

Makes 1 cup (approximately ⅓ pint/200ml)

Pour 7oz (200ml) of boiling water per serve over the blackcurrant sage or blackcurrant leaves, lemon verbena leaves, and winter savory in either the pitcher or teapot (depending on the quantity you are making). Steep for 20 minutes. Let cool and then strain into your serving cup(s).

Pineapple Sage & Scented Geranium TEA

The strong sweet aroma of pineapple sage (*Salvia elegans*) is tangy and calming. The aromatic lemony notes of scented geranium (*Pelargonium*) that I use here provide an additional complementary layer of flavor. This is a simple steeped tea that is delicious either hot or cold.

- 7oz (200ml) boiling water
- 15 pineapple sage leaves
- 4 scented geranium leaves

- **Tools:** Heatproof measuring pitcher, teapot (optional), teaspoon, tea strainer, serving cup(s)

Makes 1 cup (approximately ⅓ pint/200ml)

Geranium

Pour 7oz (200ml) of boiling water per serve over the sage and geranium leaves in either the pitcher or teapot (depending on how much you are making). Steep for 20 minutes. Let cool and then strain into your serving cup(s).

Pineapple sage is busting with anti-inflammatory, antioxidant, and antimicrobial properties. It is a source of vitamins A and K. It can relieve symptoms as varied as hot flashes (flushes), anxiety, and depression, as well as bacterial infections like sore throats. If that's not enough, it is also good for indigestion and gas. The only word of warning is to avoid pineapple sage if you are breastfeeding or pregnant because it contains thujone, which is a uterine stimulant.

HOME-MADE INGREDIENTS

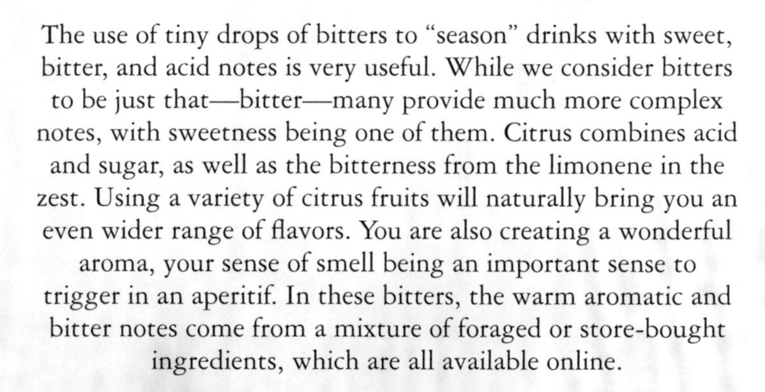

Citrus BITTERS

The use of tiny drops of bitters to "season" drinks with sweet, bitter, and acid notes is very useful. While we consider bitters to be just that—bitter—many provide much more complex notes, with sweetness being one of them. Citrus combines acid and sugar, as well as the bitterness from the limonene in the zest. Using a variety of citrus fruits will naturally bring you an even wider range of flavors. You are also creating a wonderful aroma, your sense of smell being an important sense to trigger in an aperitif. In these bitters, the warm aromatic and bitter notes come from a mixture of foraged or store-bought ingredients, which are all available online.

* Finely chopped zest of the following unwaxed, organic citrus fruits (feel free to vary the combination): 4 grapefruits, 6 lemons, 10 limes, 6 oranges, 6 bergamot lemons
* 1 tsp dried angelica root
* 1 tbsp dried hogweed (*Heracleum sphondylium*) seeds (or 1 tbsp coriander seeds)
* Large handful of herb bennet (*Geum urbanum*) roots, washed and finely chopped (or 2 allspice berries, crushed)
* 6 angelica seeds (or 6 cardamom pods)
* 1 tsp dried cut gentian root
* 1 tsp dried cut *Cinchona* bark
* 1 tsp freshly grated ginger
* 1 tsp dried field marigold (*Calendula arvensis*) leaves
* 4oz (125ml) dry Marsala wine or dry sherry
* 1¾ cups (450ml) high-proof vodka, 100 proof/50% ABV minimum (as high a proof as you can get)

Tools

* 1-quart (1-liter) wide-mouthed, sealable jar, sterilized (see page 12)
* Fine-mesh strainer and muslin/cheesecloth or coffee filter
* 4 x 5oz (150ml) or 10 x 2oz (60ml) dropper bottles, sterilized (see page 12)

Makes approximately 1 pint (500ml)

Put all the ingredients in the sterilized jar. Seal and shake the jar, then store in a cool, dark place for 1 week, tasting daily in case you get a sufficiently strong taste sooner. Fine-strain the bitters (see page 13) into a wide-mouthed pitcher and allow the contents to settle. If there is any sediment, repeat the process. Funnel the strained bitters into the sterilized bottles. Label the bottles (if you are liable to forget what is in them) and store them in a cool, dark place. Consume within 18 months.

Although you are making a far greater quantity here than you will realistically consume yourself, home-made bitters make a wonderful gift and, besides, to work with even tinier quantities would be very tricky. For the amount of work involved, you may as well share the joy!

Water KEFIR

Fermented water kefir is relatively quick to make and you can have your first kefir to drink within 72 hours. This is an inexact science, though, as the time it takes to make it depends on whether you had to rehydrate the kefir grains first, as well as on the season and ambient temperature. If you are happy to wait for a second fermentation, you can add secondary flavors such as fresh ginger, fresh or dried fruit, or garden or foraged spices. Avoid using citrus juice for a second ferment, as this leads to stringy, yeasty additions that don't lend themselves well to mocktails. However, fresh citrus juice added immediately with the kefir water is delicious—a healthy lemonade! You can also use Water Kefir in the Regal Mary Mocktail (see page 34).

You will need some water kefir cultures (also called water kefir grains). These are a form of SCOBY (Symbiotic Colony of Bacteria and Yeast), which is available online, but have a grainy, cauliflower-like appearance. The water used must be free of chlorine and fluoride, but contain the minerals found in mineral or spring water (which are lacking in filtered or distilled water). If you can't get hold of mineral or spring water, boil some tap water to remove the chlorine and let cool.

* 4 tbsp organic unrefined cane sugar
* 4 cups (1 liter) cool spring or mineral water
* 3 tbsp (45g) hydrated water kefir grains
* Fruit juice, fresh or dried fruit (such as raisins), herbs, or spices of choice, for flavoring (see *Method* for quantities)

Makes approximately 1 quart (1 liter)

Tools

* 2 x 1-quart (1-liter) wide-mouthed, sealable jars, sterilized (see page 12)
* Nonmetal stirring utensil (plastic is fine), sterilized (see page 12)
* Fermentation cover (such as a clean piece of cotton/closely woven dishtowel/T-shirt or coffee filter) and rubber band
* Plastic or bamboo sieve (avoid metal utensils)

Dissolve the sugar in a small amount of hot water in one of the sterilized jars. When it has dissolved, fill the jar with the water. Make sure the water is at room temperature (about 72°F/22°C) and no warmer. Add the water kefir grains, cover the jar with the fermentation cover, and secure with a rubber band. Leave the jar in a warm cupboard (preferably at 70–75°F/ 21–24°C) or on a countertop out of direct sunlight for 24–48 hours. The longer you leave the kefir, the more sugar will be consumed and the healthier it becomes. Any longer than 48 hours and you risk starving the grains. Stirring the grains regularly can speed up the fermentation process. When the kefir is fermented to your liking, remove the kefir grains by straining the kefir through the sieve into the second sterilized jar. Screw on the airtight lid. You now have water kefir.

To carbonate the kefir and add flavor, you'll need to do a second fermentation for another 1–3 days. Using a ratio of 80 percent water kefir to 20 percent additional juice, add your favorite fruit juice to the water kefir you've just strained. Also feel free to experiment with fresh or dried fruits, herbs, or spices at this stage. Seal the jar tightly with the airtight lid and leave in a cupboard or on the countertop away from direct sunlight for 1–3 days before drinking or refrigerating. Consume within 3 months.

Simply drink your water kefir as it is or serve with some additional fruit juice, iced herbal tea, or citrus juice and ice.

WATER KEFIR GRAINS

As soon as your water kefir grains arrive, rinse them in spring or mineral water and keep them in fresh spring or mineral water with some added sugar, as they need to feed to survive. They may take a few days to get going if you've bought them online, especially if the weather has been cold.

COCONUT WATER KEFIR

You can make Coconut Water Kefir simply by replacing the spring or mineral water in the Water Kefir recipe with coconut water. Try using this in the Strawberry Cosmo (see page 27).

Cow's Milk KEFIR

Well-fermented milk kefir has quite a strong, sour taste and can even be slightly carbonated. Shorter fermentation times result in a milder flavor. A few people have an intolerance to milk kefir, so I have only given a small-batch recipe here—you can always multiply out the ratios if you decide it's to your liking. I have also provided a recipe for Coconut Milk Kefir, in case that is more suitable for you.

* 1 tsp milk kefir grains
* 1 cup (250ml) organic whole milk (preferably non-homogenized)

Tools

* 1-quart (1-liter) wide-mouthed jar, sterilized (see page 12)
* Wooden spoon or chopstick, sterilized (see page 12)
* Fermentation cover (such as a clean piece of cotton/closely woven dishtowel/T-shirt or coffee filter) and rubber band
* Drinking straw
* Plastic or bamboo sieve (avoid metal utensils)
* Wide-mouthed glass or plastic pitcher (not metal), sterilized (see page 12)
* Sealable presentation bottle, sterilized (see page 12)

Makes approximately ½ pint (250ml)

Put the milk kefir grains in the sterilized jar, pour in the milk, and gently stir with the wooden spoon or chopstick. Cover with the fermentation cover and secure with a rubber band (the gas needs to be able to escape). Store in a cupboard or on a countertop out of direct sunlight. The warmer the location—ideally 72°F (22°C)—the quicker your kefir will ferment. Taste with a straw after 12 hours. Stir once a day to speed up the fermentation process.

The kefir should be ready within 48 hours. Your very first batch is unlikely to taste great, but don't be disheartened: the balance of yeasts and lactobacillus will improve with each batch.

Once you have a slightly thickened kefir that has just started to separate into thick curds and liquid whey, strain the contents through the sieve, stirring gently, into a wide-mouthed pitcher and then funnel into the sterilized presentation bottle. Seal and store in the refrigerator, where the kefir will ripen slowly and ferment further. Consume within 1 week.

COCONUT MILK KEFIR

Coconut milk kefir is milder and less tangy than its dairy counterpart. I use a canned organic coconut milk, which has a lusciously rich texture due to its fat content. However, you will still need milk kefir grains when making this kefir to get the fermentation process going.

Follow the instructions for the Cow's Milk Kefir, but use 1½ cups (400ml) of organic coconut milk with 1 tablespoon of milk kefir grains. The fermented coconut milk should be ready in 3 days (rather than 2 days).

Store the kefir in the refrigerator between uses, but note that the milk kefir grains will not survive in coconut milk kefir, as they require the lactose (milk sugar) in dairy milk to thrive.

So, you will need to replace the kefir grains regularly if you want to repeat the process. Consume within 1 week.

Try using this kefir in a very grown-up Vegan & Virgin Piña Colada (see page 26).

MILK KEFIR GRAINS

To revive your milk kefir grains if you've bought them online, rinse them gently with fresh milk through a plastic or bamboo sieve. Place them in milk immediately, as they need the lactose (milk sugar) to survive. They may take a few days to get going, especially if the weather is cold.

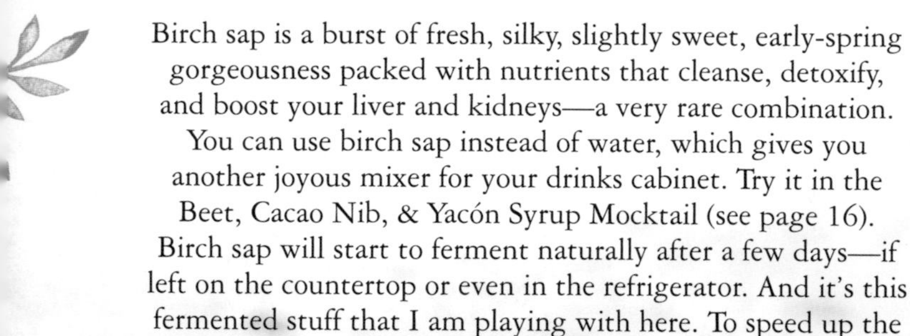

Fermented BIRCH SAP

Birch sap is a burst of fresh, silky, slightly sweet, early-spring gorgeousness packed with nutrients that cleanse, detoxify, and boost your liver and kidneys—a very rare combination. You can use birch sap instead of water, which gives you another joyous mixer for your drinks cabinet. Try it in the Beet, Cacao Nib, & Yacón Syrup Mocktail (see page 16). Birch sap will start to ferment naturally after a few days—if left on the countertop or even in the refrigerator. And it's this fermented stuff that I am playing with here. To speed up the fermentation process, simply add a handful of raisins to the birch sap. You will be left with a sour tonic that is packed with probiotics. You can also add herbs, fruits, and spices to enhance the flavor. I use the fermented tonic in the Sea Buckthorn & Fermented Birch Sap Mocktail (see page 24).

* 4 cups (1 liter) fresh birch sap (either store-bought or freshly tapped)
* A handful of raisins
* Selection of herbs, spices, and fruits of choice, for flavoring

Tools

* 1-quart (1-liter) wide-mouthed jar, sterilized (see page 12)
* Fermentation cover (such as a clean piece of cotton/closely woven dishtowel/T-shirt or coffee filter) and rubber band
* Fine-mesh strainer and muslin/cheesecloth or coffee filter
* Sealable presentation bottle(s), sterilized (see page 12)

Makes approximately 1 quart (1 liter)

Pour your birch sap into the sterilized jar and add the raisins to speed up the fermentation. Add your choice of herbs, fruits, or spices to enhance the flavor. Cover the jar with the fermentation cover and secure with a rubber band. Leave at room temperature for 2 days. Fine-strain the fermented birch sap (see page 13) into a wide-mouthed pitcher and funnel into the sterilized presentation bottle(s). Keep in the refrigerator and consume within 1 week.

HOW TO TAP BIRCH SAP

For anyone who has not sampled the joys of birch tapping in very early spring, I thoroughly recommend it. All species of birch can be tapped, the most common being the white birch (*Betula alba*) and the silver birch (*Betula pendula*). Alternatively, fresh birch sap is available from some health-food and grocery stores, although you won't enjoy the romance of tapping your own.

1 Wait until temperatures start rising above freezing (early spring in the U.K.) and find a birch tree with a diameter of at least 10in (25cm)—the more branches the tree has, the better the sap will flow.

2 Make a natural tap from a piece of shaved twig for directing the sap into a plastic collecting container (such as a bottle). You can also use food-grade tubing instead of a twig. Find a spot on the trunk, about 3ft (1m) above the ground. Tie the container to the tree at this point and wedge the twig tap or tubing inside so the sap will run into it. (Cover open containers, as the sap will attract insects.)

3 Drive a sharp knife into the tree at an upward angle, just above the collecting container, to a depth of about 1½in (4cm). Create a small flap in the bark and then use the twig tap or tubing to direct the sap into the container.

The water-like sap should start flowing and collecting in the container almost immediately. You can leave the container attached to the tree until the flow of sap slows down or starts turning cloudy (which indicates that the window of opportunity has closed). Only tap a maximum of 1 gallon (3.5 liters) of sap—this will take about a day. The birch-tapping season only lasts 2–3 weeks.

4 At the end of the session, carefully remove the twig tap or tubing, and press down hard on the flap of raised birch bark to close the slit as best you can. The birch tree will then do the rest to seal and heal the bark.

Strawberry, Clover, & Meadowsweet SHRUB

The sweetness of strawberries and red clover (*Trifolium pratense*) combined with the almond-y, honey flavor of meadowsweet (*Filipendula ulmaria*) flowers and the aromatics of meadowsweet seeds make for a delicious shrub. Strawberries are well known for their vitamin C content and high antioxidant levels. The unfiltered apple cider vinegar is packed with potassium and live enzymes, and helps to promote youthful skin, regulate calcium metabolism, lower blood pressure and cholesterol, aid digestion, and reduce chronic fatigue. It can also aid weight control. Not bad results from one ingredient! Letting the shrub ferment gently over a few days means it can also improve your digestion and help colonize your gut with healthy bacteria. Try this shrub in the Fruity and Flowery Summer Mocktail (see page 28).

* 4 heads of meadowsweet blossoms, fully opened
* 2 cups (400g) chopped organic strawberries
* ½ cup (about 15–20) red clover flowers
* 2 tsp meadowsweet seeds, if you have any from last year (optional)
* 1 cup (320g) raw, runny honey
* 1 cup (250ml) white balsamic vinegar
* 1 cup (250ml) organic, raw, unfiltered apple cider vinegar

Tools

1-quart (1-liter) wide-mouthed, sealable jar, with a nonreactive lid, sterilized (see page 12)

* Wooden spoon or muddler
* Fine-mesh strainer and muslin/cheesecloth or coffee filter
* Sealable presentation bottle(s), with nonreactive lid(s), sterilized (see page 12)

Makes approximately 1 pint (500ml)

Strip the meadowsweet blossoms of stems and stalks, and set them aside in order to give the wildlife plenty of time to disperse.

Put the strawberries in the sterilized jar. Add the clover and meadowsweet flowers, and meadowsweet seeds (if using). Using the end of the wooden spoon or muddler, lightly crush the fruit, blossoms, and seeds.

Add the honey and vinegars, and stir thoroughly to combine. It is important that you cover the jar with a glass or plastic (i.e. nonreactive) lid. Alternatively, if you are using a canning jar that has a metal lid, put a piece of parchment or waxed paper between the vinegar and the lid, to prevent it from corroding. Put the sealed jar in the refrigerator to infuse for 1 week, shaking gently every day.

Fine-strain the shrub (see page 13) into a wide-mouthed pitcher and funnel into the sterilized presentation bottle(s). Store in the refrigerator and consume within 6 months.

To create a delicious drink, simply mix ½–1oz (15–30ml) of the shrub with 8oz (240ml) sparkling water in an ice-filled highball glass.

Coumarin, the slightly vanilla-flavored phytochemical found in red clover, meadowsweet, sweet woodruff (*Galium odoratum*), and cleavers (*Galium aparine*), has antifungal and antitumor properties. It also thins the blood, especially if it is dried in damp conditions. However, you should only consume it in moderation and avoid it altogether if you are taking anticoagulants.

FLAVORED SYRUPS

Infusing a simple syrup with fresh ingredients gives a mocktail or cocktail outstanding flavor and sweetness. As with all elements of cocktail mixology, you will find a host of methods claiming to be the best. The recipes on the following pages use a hot, or rapid, infusion technique for great results, achieved very quickly and easily. A cold infusion (maceration) or a sous vide method (using a vacuum-sealed bag in a water bath) to extract the flavors at a specific low temperature (around 140°F/60°C) can result in a brighter, clearer syrup of outstanding purity, but life may be just a little too short if you are doing this for fun. The joy of making flavored syrups is that you can drink them on their own as a soda, with lots of ice and water, or incorporate them into a drink of your choice.

Ginger SYRUP

This syrup will come in handy, not just for your mocktails and cocktails, but also for a variety of gastronomic delights like marinades, stir fries, and desserts.

* 2 cups (400g) superfine (caster) sugar
* 2 cups (500ml) water
* 2½oz (75g) fresh ginger, fairly thickly sliced
* 1 tbsp fresh lemon juice or 80 proof/40% ABV vodka (optional)

* **Tools:** Sealable presentation bottle(s), sterilized (see page 12)

Makes approximately 1 pint (500ml)

Place the sugar and water in a nonreactive pan and slowly bring to a boil. Add the ginger and let simmer for 5 minutes. Remove from the heat and let the ginger steep for another 10 minutes.

Strain the syrup into a wide-mouthed pitcher and then funnel into the sterilized presentation bottle(s) and seal. Store in the refrigerator and consume within 2 weeks. A tablespoon of lemon juice or high-proof vodka added just after removing the pan from the heat will increase the shelf life of the syrup for up to a month.

Once you have made the syrup, sprinkle the ginger slices on top of vanilla ice cream to make a grown-up dessert, or dip them in granulated sugar, for candied ginger, which you can serve on its own as candy or as a pretty mocktail garnish.

Honeysuckle SYRUP

A hedgerow or wall covered in wild honeysuckle (*Lonicera periclymenum*) is a heady and erotic feast for the senses. *Lonicera japonica* is equally sweet and delicious and, like wild honeysuckle, can be found naturalized across Europe and North America, scrambling over gardens, walls, and wasteland. Honeysuckle has the strongest scent at night, so try to harvest unopened and newly opened flowers during the evening or early morning.

* 8 large handfuls of unsprayed honeysuckle flowers, leaves and stems removed
* Approximately 2 cups (400g) superfine (caster) sugar
* Freshly squeezed juice of ½ lemon

* **Tools:** Sealable presentation bottle(s), sterilized (see page 12)

Makes approximately 1 pint (500ml)

Place the honeysuckle flowers in a nonreactive bowl and cover with cold water, then steep for 12 hours, or at least overnight, at room temperature. Make sure the flowers are completely covered by the water.

Strain the mixture into a measuring cup, discarding the flowers. Pour the liquid into a nonreactive pan. Measure an equal amount of sugar to the liquid and add to the pan. Bring to a boil, and let simmer for 5 minutes. Feel free to replace half the sugar with a handful of chopped sweet cicely leaves, but bear in mind that this will adjust the color.

Remove from the heat, let cool, add the lemon juice, and funnel into the sterilized presentation bottle(s).

There is some debate about the toxicity of certain species of honeysuckle, their berries in particular, so stick to *Lonicera periclymenum* and *L. japonica*, and leave the berries alone.

Mahonia SYRUP

Mahonias are as tough as old boots and provide year-round interest with their racemes of yellow flowers, followed by amazing purple berries, which resemble grapes. Instead of picking berries from shrubs in public spaces, which could have been sprayed with pesticides or be full of carbon monoxide, I prefer to ask people if I can pick a few from their yard. This syrup is superb in an Only the Mahonia (see page 38).

* 4 cups (500g) ripe mahonia (*M. japonica* or *M. aquifolium*) berries
* 2 cups (500ml) water
* 2 cups (400g) superfine (caster) sugar

* **Tools:** Sealable, heatproof presentation bottle(s) or jars, sterilized (see page 12)

Makes approximately 1 pint (500ml)

Remove the berries from their stem and rinse them. Place them in a nonreactive pan with the water and heat slowly. The water will change to dark purple. As soon as the water starts to bubble, remove the pan, gently mash the berries and strain into a wide-mouthed measuring cup. Pour into a clean nonreactive pan. For each cup (250ml) of liquid, measure out the same amount of sugar and add to the pan. Bring to a boil over a medium heat, then simmer for 5 minutes. While the liquid is still piping hot, funnel into the bottle(s) or jar(s), seal, and store in the refrigerator for up to 2 weeks.

Both species are great for making syrups but *M. aquifolium* make an attractive garnish too. Be warned: as you pick the berries, your hands, and everything you touch, will start to run with a blood-colored juice.

Meadowsweet SYRUP

Interspersed with pink and purple wild vetches and peas, meadowsweet (*Filipendula ulmaria*) blossom is a beautiful sight, and the heady, almondy, vanilla, and honey scent is easily transferred to an exquisite syrup.

* 15 heads of meadowsweet blossoms, fully opened
* 4 cups (1 liter) water
* 5 cups (1kg) superfine (caster) sugar
* Zest and juice of 1 unwaxed, organic lemon

* **Tools:** Sealable presentation bottle(s), sterilized (see page 12)

Makes approximately 1 quart (1 liter)

Meadowsweet

The leaves and stalks taste vegetal and medicinal when boiled, so strip the flowers from their stalks with your fingers or a fork before adding them to the pan.

Make a simple syrup by heating the sugar and water in a nonreactive pan over a low heat, stirring to dissolve the sugar. Once it reaches boiling point, remove the pan from the heat. Add the lemon zest and flowers. Submerge the flowers in the syrup, cover, and leave overnight or up to 12 hours, to infuse.

Add the lemon juice, stir, then strain into a wide-mouthed pitcher to remove the flowers and lemon zest. Reheat the syrup gently in a clean nonreactive pan and funnel into the sterilized presentation bottle(s) while still piping hot. Seal the bottle.

Store somewhere cool and dark. Once opened, keep in the refrigerator for 2 to 3 months.

PLANTS

Aloysia citrodora

LEMON VERBENA

A native of South America, lemon verbena is a deciduous sub-shrub with aromatic leaves and tiny white or pale lilac flowers.

Taste profile: Incredible lemony scent and taste that intensifies when the leaves are touched or bruised.

Store-bought alternatives: Mint or lemons

Berberis darwinii

DARWIN'S BARBERRY

This dense, medium-sized evergreen shrub has dark, glossy green, broadly oblong, sparsely spined leaves and drooping racemes of rich orange flowers, tinged red in bud, followed by blue-black berries.

Taste profile: Young flowers taste like delicious, tropical/floral, sweet/sour fruit. When fully ripe, the fruit loses most of its acidity and is sweet.

Store-bought alternative: None

Cydonia oblonga

QUINCE

Belonging to the same family as apples and pears, quince are shaped like pears, but are larger. Native to Southwest Asia, they have lumpy, yellow skin and a hard flesh that is inedible unless cooked, although you can infuse raw quince dipped in lemon in alcohol.

Taste profile: When cooked, tastes like a floral, perfume-y apple or pear crossed with melon.

Store-bought alternative: Pears

Filipendula ulmaria

MEADOWSWEET

A mid-summer-flowering perennial herb with clouds of creamy, fluffy blossom that smells of almonds, honey, and vanilla. It is native to most of Europe and western Asia, but has naturalized in North America and New Zealand.

Taste profile: This aromatic plant is high in essential oils, which gives it a strong, heady scent. Young meadowsweet buds taste of pure marzipan when chewed raw. The dried leaves smell like hay, because they contain coumarin (dry the leaves quickly to avoid creating a mold that can turn the coumarin into a toxic compound). Meadowsweet is also astringent and contains a significant amount of tannins.

Store-bought alternative: Orgeat syrup (for an almond taste

Foeniculum vulgare

WILD FENNEL

A tall, hardy perennial, native to Europe, with striking, feathery, green leaves and yellow flowers in large umbels in late summer. The flowers are followed by delicious, aniseed-scented seeds in the fall (autumn).

Taste profile: The leaves have a perfume-y, anise-like flavor, while fennel pollen has a concentrated floral, citrus, and sweet-anise flavor. The seeds have a woodsy, earthy, anise flavor.

Store-bought alternative: None

Fragaria

STRAWBERRY

This fleshy, juicy, summer fruit grows from runners/stolons, which put down new roots to produce cloned plants.

Taste profile: Sweet, jammy, juicy, fresh, rosy, floral.

Store-bought alternatives: Plenty available

Lavandula

LAVENDER

This small evergreen shrub, with aromatic leaves, is largely native to northern Africa and the mountainous regions of the Mediterranean.

Taste profile: Floral, pungent aroma; earthy, with an undertone of mint.

Store-bought alternative: Commercial lavender

Mahonia aquifolium

OREGON GRAPE

This shade-loving evergreen shrub has large clusters of yellow flowers in spring, followed by amazing blue/purple berries that resemble grapes in the fall (autumn). *M. japonica* (Japanese mahonia) is also evergreen, with sprays of fragrant, light yellow flowers and blue/black berries.

Taste profile: The berries taste very sharp and need some sort of sweetening. The flowers are ridiculously delicious eaten raw when young—sweet/sour, almost like honey with a citrus tang—and with an exquisite scent. The perfect garnish.

Store-bought alternative: None

Matricaria discoidea

PINEAPPLE WEED

A perennial herb native to most parts of the northern and southern hemispheres, including Australia and New Zealand. The leaves have a feathery, chamomile-like appearance. The flowers appear once the summer heat really gets going and are daisy-like, with white petals that do not last long. The inner yellow/green corollas are dome-shaped.

Taste profile: The flowerheads smell and taste strongly of pineapple. The later in the season you pick them, the more bitter the aftertaste.

Store-bought alternative: None

Melissa officinalis

LEMON BALM

Perennial herbaceous herb native to the southern Mediterranean, the Middle East, and parts of central Asia. Also naturalized elsewhere.

Taste profile: Lemon

Store-bought alternative: Mint

Myrrhis odorata

SWEET CICELY

An aromatic herbaceous perennial, native to Europe, with gorgeous, fern-like leaves in spring and umbels of small, white flowers in early summer. These are followed by long, thin, aniseed-scented, brown-ribbed seeds in late summer. You might get new growth again in the fall (autumn). Not to be confused with the *Osmorhiza* genus, which is native to Asia and the American continents, and also called "sweet cicely."

Taste profile: The leaves, seeds, and roots have a strong, sweet, anise flavor. Great with rhubarb.

Store-bought alternatives: Fennel, licorice

Salvia microphylla

BLACKCURRANT SAGE

An evergreen member of the sage family that is native to Arizona and Mexico. It has beautiful, blackcurrant-scented leaves and striking cerise flowers.

Taste profile: Strong scent and taste of blackcurrant from the leaves; the flowers just look good!

Store-bought alternative: Blackcurrants

Syringa vulgaris

LILAC

Spring-flowering woody shrub or small tree covered in panicles of heavily fragrant blossom that is usually purple or mauve, but can also be white or pink. Native to the Balkan Peninsula.

Taste profile: An intoxicatingly floral and sweet scent and taste when used in syrups and teas. The raw lilac blossoms are bitter, floral, and astringent.

Store-bought alternative: None

Trifolium pratense

RED CLOVER

A short biennial or perennial, native to Europe and northern Asia, with red, pink, or pinkish-purple flowerheads.

Taste profile: Sweet-tasting. Needs a long infusion (20–30 minutes) to draw out the sweet and savory notes—like floral, honey-roasted vegetables!

Store-bought alternative: None

Tropaeolum majus

NASTURTIUM

A sprawling annual, from Bolivia to Colombia, with bright orange/red/yellow flowers and circular green leaves with star-shaped veins.

Taste profile: Mustard and pepper in both the leaves and flowers.

Store-bought alternative: Mustard leaves

INDEX

PICTURE CREDITS

All photography by Kim Lightbody except for pp. 4–5, 12–15 (background), 20, 26, 27, 54–55 (background) Mowie Kay; pp. 19, 40 Adrian Lawrence; p. 13 William Lingwood; p. 41, bottom William Reavell; pp. 34 bottom left, 35, 61–64 (background) Christopher Scholey; pp. 32, 36 Kate Whitaker; pp. 22, 23, 44, 57 Clare Winfield